GA

CENGAGE Learning

C000001570

Drama for Students, Volume 10

Staff

Series Editors: Michael L. LaBlanc.

Contributing Editors: Elizabeth Bellalouna, Anne Marie Hacht, Ira Mark Milne, Jennifer Smith.

Managing Editor: Dwayne Hayes.

Research: Victoria B. Cariappa, *Research Team Manager*. Maureen Eremic, Barb McNeil, Cheryl Warnock, *Research Specialists*. Andy Malonis, *Technical Training Specialist*. Barbara Leevy, Tamara Nott, Tracie A. Richardson, Robert Whaley, *Research Associates*. Scott Floyd, Nicodemus Ford, Sarah Genik, Timothy Lehnerer, *Research Assistants*.

Permissions: Maria Franklin, *Permissions Manager*. Margaret A. Chamberlain, Edna Hedblad, *Permissions Specialists*. Erin Bealmear, Shalice Shah-Caldwell, Sarah Tomasek, *Permissions*

Associates. Debra Freitas, Julie Juengling, Mark Plaza, *Permissions Assistants*.

Manufacturing: Mary Beth Trimper, *Manager, Composition and Electronic Prepress*. Evi Seoud, *Assistant Manager, Composition Purchasing and Electronic Prepress*. Stacy Melson, *Buyer*.

Imaging and Multimedia Content Team: Randy Bassett, *Image Database Supervisor*. Robert Duncan, Dan Newell, *Imaging Specialists*. Pamela A. Reed, *Imaging Coordinator*. Dean Dauphinais, Robyn V. Young, *Senior Image Editors*. Kelly A. Quin, *Image Editor*.

Product Design Team: Kenn Zorn, *Product Design Manager*. Pamela A. E. Galbreath, *Senior Art Director*. Michael Logusz, *Graphic Artist*.

of the publisher and verified to the satisfaction of the publisher will be corrected in future editions.

© 2001 Gale Group, Inc.
27500 Drake Rd.
Farmington Hills, MI 48331–3535

Gale Group and Design is a trademark used herein under license.

This book is printed on acid-free paper that meets the minimum requirements of American National Standard for Information Sciences—Permanence Paper for Printed Library Materials, ANSI Z39.48-1984.

ISBN 0-7876-4084-0
ISSN 1094-9232

Printed in Canada
10 9 8 7 6 5 4 3 2 1

Death and the King's Horseman

Wole Soyinka

1975

Introduction

Death and the King's Horseman is considered by many to be among the best of Wole Soyinka's plays, which number more than a dozen. In awarding Soyinka the Nobel Prize for Literature in 1986, the Swedish Academy drew special attention to *Death and the King's Horseman* and *Dance of the Forests*(1960) as evidence of his talent for combining Yoruban and European culture into a unique kind of poetic drama.

Death and the King's Horseman play tells the story of Elesin, the king's horseman, who is expected to commit ritual suicide following the death of the king, but who is distracted from his duty. The story is based on a historical event. In 1946, a royal horseman named Elesin was prevented from committing ritual suicide by the British colonial powers. Soyinka alters the historical facts, placing the responsibility for Elesin's failure squarely on Elesin's shoulders, so that he might focus on the theme of duty rather than of colonialism.

The play is well known in the United States, frequently anthologized in textbooks as an example of African drama for students and teachers who are increasingly curious about the literature of other parts of the world. Because of its mingling of Western and Yoruban elements, and because of the universality of its theme of cultural responsibility, *Death and the King's Horseman* is seen as a good introduction to African thought and tradition. While it is frequently read, however, the play is seldom performed outside of Africa. Soyinka himself has directed important American productions, in Chicago in 1976 and at Lincoln Center in New York in 1987, but these productions were more admired than loved. Although respected by critics, Soyinka's plays are challenging for Westerners to perform and to understand, and they have not been popular successes.

Author Biography

Akinwande Oluwole Soyinka was born in Ijebu Isara, near Akeokuta in western Nigeria, on July 13, 1934. His parents, who were from different Yoruba-speaking ethnic groups, were Christians, but other relatives observed African beliefs and deities. Nigeria was at the time a colony of Great Britain. Soyinka grew up, therefore, with exposure to both Yoruban and Western culture. At twenty he left Nigeria to attend the University of Leeds in England, a university with a strong drama program. After graduation he joined London's Royal Court Theatre as a script-reader and then as a writer, and produced his first play, *The Swamp Dwellers,* there in 1959.

The next year Nigeria gained independence. Soyinka returned to his homeland, where the Arts Theatre in Ibadan had begun presenting plays by Nigerian playwrights, on Nigerian themes, for Nigerian audiences. Soyinka traveled throughout Nigeria, absorbing all he could of the Yoruba people's rich oral literature, graphic art, dance, and pageantry. He created plays incorporating traditional Yoruban dance, music, and proverbs with political messages about the need for Nigerians to break free from the influences of Western culture. His third play, *A Dance of the Forests*(1960), is typical of Soyinka's early work in several ways: it deals with conflicts between African and colonial values, it is written in English but includes Yoruban materials, and its first productions featured Soyinka as author, producer, director, and performer.

Independent Nigeria has been a troubled country, headed by greedy and corrupt leaders. In 1965, Soyinka was arrested for criticizing the government over the radio, but he was acquitted. In 1967 he criticized the government in print, and was arrested again. This time he was held prisoner without charges for more than two years, spending fifteen months in solitary confinement. After his prison experiences, his work became more political and more strident. In many of his newer plays, he turned his critical gaze away from British colonialism and toward corrupt African leaders. Other plays, including *Death and the King's Horseman*(1975), examine weaknesses in Nigerian society as a whole, caused by individuals forgetting their traditions, their culture, and their duty to themselves and to each other.

Soyinka has written more than a dozen plays, as well as poetry, criticism, and an autobiography. In 1986 he became the first African writer to win the Nobel Prize for Literature. The award increased his international stature and widened the audience for his political messages. Within Nigeria, Soyinka is a well-known intellectual and political activist, speaking and writing against government corruption. The government has made its displeasure clear, and Soyinka lived in the United States for a few years during the late 1990s after being accused of treason. "Some people think the Nobel Prize makes you bulletproof," he said in an interview with Ciugu Mwagiru. "I never had that illusion."

Plot Summary

Act I

As *Death and the King's Horseman* opens, Elesin Oba walks through a Nigerian village market at the close of the business day. He is followed by an entourage of drummers and praise-singers, and as he makes his way through the market he talks with the praise-singer Olohun-iyo about "the other side" and about the importance of "this day of all days." Apparently, Elesin Oba is enjoying his last day on earth; at night he will go to join his "great forebears." The women abandon their work of putting away the goods from their stalls and come to flirt with Elesin, who is obviously a great favorite and well known for his sexual prowess and his many conquests.

Much of the dialogue is written in rhythmic free verse. Elesin dances, and chants the story of the Not-I bird, a bird who fails to fulfill his duty. In an exchange with the crowd, laced with Yoruba proverbs, Elesin promises that when the time comes to fulfill his duty he will not delay. Led by Iyaloja, the mother of the market, the women dress Elesin in their richest cloths and dance around him. Suddenly he is distracted by the sight of a beautiful woman whom he has never seen before. Although she is already engaged to someone else, Elesin demands that he be allowed to take her to bed before he dies.

Because Elesin is at the threshold between life and death, he cannot be refused. Iyaloja warns him not to be deterred from his duty, and not to bring trouble on the people who will remain. Then, as the other women prepare the young woman to be Elesin's bride, Iyaloja leaves to prepare the bridal bed.

Act II

This act occurs during the same evening, at the home of the district officer, Simon Pilkings, a British officer stationed in the British colony of Nigeria. Simon and his wife, Jane, are listening to a tango, dancing in the shadows. Amusa, a Nigerian working for the British as a native administration policeman, arrives and is horrified to see that Simon and Jane are dressed in the clothing traditionally worn for the *egungun* ceremony, costumes sacred to members of a local religious cult. Simon has confiscated the robes from the cult leaders, and he and Jane plan to wear them to win a prize for best costume at a fancy-dress ball the British are holding that night. Although Amusa is a Muslim and not a part of the cult, he respects the clothes and will not speak to Simon until he has removed them.

Amusa and the house-servant Joseph explain that Elesin will commit ritual suicide that night. The *alafin* or king of Elesin's people died one month before, but has not yet been buried. According to "native law and custom" Elesin, as the king's chief horseman, must kill himself that night so the king will not be alone. Simon and Jane discuss the foolishness of native belief, and remember proudly that Simon helped Elesin's oldest son, Olunde, leave the village to attend medical school in England, against his father's wishes. Simon also reveals a surprise: the prince of England will be at the ball. Although Simon does not care personally what happens to Elesin, he cannot afford to have any trouble while the prince is visiting his district. To prevent Elesin's death, Simon orders him arrested.

Act III

The third Act returns to the market, where one of the stalls has been converted into a wedding chamber. Amusa and two constables are attempting to arrest Elesin, but the women stand around them hurling insults, claiming that working for the white man has cost Amusa his manhood. The women grab the men's hats and batons, do a mocking imitation of British officers, and send the men away.

Elesin emerges from the wedding chamber, and shows Iyaloja the stained cloth that proves that the bride was a virgin. As he makes plans for his final moments on earth, he listens to the sound of the ritual drumming; he can tell that the king's horse and dog have already been killed, and that soon it will be his turn to die. As he listens to the drums, he falls into a state of semi-hypnosis, and begins his passage to the next world. He dances, his limbs becoming heavier and heavier, as the praise-singer calls out to him, wishing Elesin could stay.

Act IV

The fourth Act opens at the home of the resident, the British chief officer, as the prince enters the ballroom accompanied by an orchestra playing "Rule Britannia." The prince admires Simon and Jane's *egungun* attire, then joins the dancing. Alerted by Amusa, Simon and the resident have a whispered conference in the hallway. Simon tells his superior about the "strange custom" that Elesin will be prevented from carrying out, and the men agree that there must be no trouble while the prince is visiting. Realizing that it is midnight, Simon leaves hurriedly for the marketplace, leaving Jane to enjoy the rest of the ball.

As soon as Simon is gone, Elesin's son Olunde steps from the shadows to speak with Jane. He gently rebukes her for wearing the sacred *egungun* garments for a trivial purpose. He thinks the British are disrespectful people, but praises the courage British men have shown in fighting the Second World War, which is raging in Europe but almost unnoticed in Nigeria. Olunde needs to speak with Simon, and asks for Jane's help in finding him. Word reached Olunde in England that the king has died, and Olunde knows that on this night he will be called as oldest son to bury his father. He also knows that Simon will try to prevent Elesin's suicide, and he wants to stop Simon from making this mistake. He tries to explain to Jane that the tradition is sacred, and that it holds the universe on course even if she and Simon cannot understand it. He can calmly accept his father's death, because he knows it is necessary.

Simon returns, and Olunde thanks him for not interfering. But there is a commotion outside, and Olunde hears Elesin's voice. Elesin is alive, shouting accusations at the white men who have brought him shame. Against all propriety, the father and son see each other, something they are forbidden to do once the king is dead. Disgusted by Elesin's failure, Olunde says, "I have no father" and walks away.

Act V

The final Act is set in Elesin's prison cell. Simon comments on the peaceful night, but Elesin corrects him, telling him that because the ritual has not been enacted the world will never know peace again. Simon cannot understand the importance of Elesin's failure, and rejects any suggestion that something is amiss. The two discuss Olunde's fate. Simon is sure that Olunde will return to England to continue his studies. Elesin is proud that his son, who had seemed to reject his own culture, was man enough to reject him. Iyaloja comes to Elesin, reminding him of her earlier warning. She knows that Elesin, not Simon, is at fault for not carrying out his suicide, because he allowed himself to be distracted by the young woman, and Elesin accepts the blame. Iyaloja reveals that she has brought "a burden": the body of Olunde, who has killed himself in his father's place. When he sees his son, Elesin manages to strangle himself with his chains. The bride does her wifely duty, closing Elesin's eyes with dirt, then leaves with Iyaloja, who counsels her, "Now forget the dead, forget even the living. Turn your mind only to the unborn."

Characters

Amusa

Amusa is a sergeant in the native administration police, a black African working for the white British colonialists. His position is a difficult one: he is not trusted by Simon Pilkings, his superior, because Simon cannot conceive of an African as being intelligent or honest, and he is no longer trusted by the villagers because he works with the whites to enforce "the laws of strangers." Amusa was converted to Christianity two years before the play begins, but he still feels profound respect for native beliefs. He will not speak with Simon so long as Simon is wearing the *egungun* garments, but Amusa does not hesitate to follow Simon's orders and arrest Elesin to prevent his suicide.

Bride

The Bride does not speak at all during the play. Already engaged to Iyaloja's son, the Bride is seen by Elesin and taken to bed by him; no one asks for her consent. When Elesin is arrested she sits silently beside him, and upon his death she closes his eyes in fulfillment of her wifely duty.

Iyaloja

Iyaloja is the Mother of the market, the spokesperson and leader of the women of the village. She is the voice of wisdom in the play, the one who can see beyond Elesin's charms to the danger he represents when he swerves from his responsibility. When Elesin asks for the young woman as his Bride, Iyaloja has no choice but to hand her over, even though the young woman is engaged to Iyaloja's own son. Iyaloja knows the power of the forces of the universe, and she understands that refusing the request of a man who is "already touched by the waiting fingers of our departed" will "set this world adrift." But she warns Elesin not to leave a cursed seed behind him, and she reminds him of her warning when she brings Olunde's body to Elesin's cell.

Elesin Oba

Elesin Oba, a man of "enormous vitality," was the chief horseman of the dead king. As the king's companion, Elesin enjoyed a luxurious life of rich food and fine clothing, the rewards of a man of his position. He enjoyed that life, and now that the king has been dead for a month and is ready for burial Elesin is expected to complete the horseman's duty and commit ritual suicide. The play opens on the evening of Elesin's last day of life; at midnight he will die. He says repeatedly that he is ready to give his life, and he knows the importance of fulfilling his responsibility. But Elesin, well known for his many sexual conquests, sees a young woman of great beauty and demands that he be allowed to take her to bed before he dies. Just after leaving the wedding chamber, Elesin begins his passage into the next world, and dances in a hypnotic dream-like trance. But when Simon's men come to arrest Elesin, he cannot summon the strength to resist them and continue through the transitional state into the next world. Instead, he lives, and brings shame to himself and chaos to the world.

Olohun-iyo

See The Praise-Singer

Jane Pilkings

Jane is the wife of Simon Pilkings, the British district officer. Although she shares most of Simon's superior attitudes, she is, in Olunde's words, "somewhat more understanding" than her husband. Unlike Simon, she can sense that Simon has offended Amusa and Joseph (the house servant), although she agrees with Simon that the native customs and beliefs are "horrible." She has no active role in the main events of the play, but serves as a sounding board for Simon as he thinks things through.

Simon Pilkings

Simon is the district officer, charged with maintaining order in the one district of the British colony of Nigeria. He has no interest in learning about the Africans and their culture. He and his wife

Jane socialize only with other Europeans, who have tried to transplant as much of their own food, clothing, and manners as they can to maintain their own style of life in a foreign country. Simon is sure of himself and of his way of life, and easily dismisses anything he does not understand. When he learns that Elesin intends to commit suicide on the night of the prince's visit to the district, Simon uses his authority to stop Elesin not because he values Elesin, but because he does not want any commotion to disrupt a fancydress ball and the prince's visit. Ironically, the steps Simon takes to ensure peace in the village actually help bring about chaos in the universe. Because he does not care to understand Yoruba belief, his actions do more harm than good.

Media Adaptations

- *Death and the King's Horseman* has not been filmed or recorded.

Praise-Singer

The Praise-Singer (also known as Olohun-iyo) accompanies Elesin on his last journey, singing and chanting. He is devoted to Elesin, and sees into the darkest corners of his heart. Almost like a conscience, he voices Elesin's hesitations and questions about his passage into the next world. As Elesin enters his trance to begin the transition, the Praise-Singer monitors his progress. He can sense Elesin moving away from him, and calls him back in a ritual, repetitive chant. Once Elesin is arrested and brought to his cell, the Praise-Singer is not seen nor heard again.

Themes

Life Cycle

Like many African cultures, the Yoruba have a fundamental belief that life is a continuum. The dead are not forgotten; the ancestors are honored and cherished as guides and companions. The not-yet-born are also cherished, and new babies may in fact be ancestors returning to physical life. The most highly charged moments in the life cycle are the moments of transition from one type of existence to the next that is, the passage into the physical world during birth and the passage into death. Elesin's responsibility as king's horseman is to enact the transition from life into death in a ritual manner, to remind the entire community through his death that life is a continuum.

Topics for Further Study

- Research the involvement of African nations in World War II. Where on the African continent were battles fought? Which nations were involved in the fighting? Does it seem reasonable that the characters in *Death and the King's Horseman* would be largely oblivious to the war? How accurate and appropriate is the term "world war"?

- The British used to have a proud saying: "The sun never sets on the British Empire." Using research and a map of the world, identify the parts of the world that were under British rule in the early 1940s, when *Death and the King's Horseman* takes place. Then identify the parts of the world under British rule in 1975, when the play was written. Where does the British Empire reach today?

- Soyinka was raised as a Christian, but his parents were also Yoruba. What evidence of this rich combination of influences is found in *Death and the King's Horseman*

- Find audio recordings of the kinds of music that are heard in this play: a tango, a Viennese waltz, the song

"Rule Britannia," and indigenous Yoruba music. How does each type of music reflect the culture that produced it?

- Research masquerade rituals performed in West Africa, paying special attention to the traditional clothing, masks, and other objects associated with these ceremonies. How are they alike and unlike the ceremonies performed in your own religious or ethnic practice?

The idea of death is found throughout the play. Elesin and the women of the village are preparing for his death. The clothing that the Pilkingses wear to the ball has been taken away from a group performing the *egungun* celebration, a ritual in which men dress as the ancestors and mingle with the living. The masqueraders take the ritual seriously, as a reminder that the ancestors are always present, and even the Muslim Amusa has respect for the stolen garments. Simon and Jane, however, cannot understand the calm acceptance of death demonstrated by the Yoruba or the respect shown for the ancestors. They perform a mocking imitation of the *egungun* ceremony, they try to prevent Elesin from dying, and they find Olunde "callous" and "unfeeling" because he does not mourn his father's death.

As a person in transition, Elesin has special

powers and special rights. His request for the Bride, although unexpected, must be granted, because "the claims of one whose foot is on the threshold of their abode surpasses even the claims of blood." Iyaloja realizes that the child born of Elesin and the Bride will be extraordinary, "neither of this world nor of the next. Nor of the one behind us. As if the timelessness of the ancestor world and the unborn have joined spirits."

Elesin, of course, does not complete his transition. Olunde dies in his place and Elesin, seeing the chaos demonstrated by the father and son reversing roles, kills himself. Simon and Jane are horrified, but Iyaloja and the Bride are placid and accepting. Iyaloja rebukes Simon for his panic, and the Bride "walks calmly into the cell" to close Elesin's eyes in the appropriate, ritual manner. The last line of the play, spoken to the Bride by Iyaloja, repeats the idea of the continuum of life: "Now forget the dead, forget even the living. Turn your mind only to the unborn."

Culture Clash

Westerners who come to *Death and the King's Horseman* without much knowledge about Yoruba culture and belief are apt to focus on the theme of the clash of cultures. Clearly, two cultures, Yoruba and British, are uneasily occupying the same geographic space, although their emotional and spiritual worlds could not be further apart. During Acts 2 and 4, for example, the British listen to a tango and orchestral music, while the sound of African drumming is continually heard in the background. Both communities call their members together during the same evening: The British hold a fancy-dress ball with the prince in attendance, and the Yoruba gather for the ritual suicide of the king's richly robed horseman and the burial of the king and his entourage. Although the differences are interesting to observe, the two communities do not enrich each other, but remain apart.

Simon and Jane Pilkings do not understand the beliefs of the Africans, and they dismiss what they do not understand as "nonsense," and as "barbaric" and "horrible custom." They see no harm in wearing the sacred *egungun* garments to a costume party and mocking the ceremonial dance, even after Amusa and Olunde point out the disrespect in their actions. Elesin's sense of tradition is so important to him that he is willing to die for it. By contrast, Simon's Christianity seems to mean little to Simon, who mocks Joseph for his devout faith in "that holy water nonsense." Nevertheless, this man of little faith feels qualified to label Elesin an "old pagan." Simon does not understand or respect Elesin's culture, and he uses his authority to interfere only because he does not want to be embarrassed while the prince is visiting.

It is tempting, therefore, to see Simon as the cause of Elesin's not fulfilling his duty, to see the clash of cultures as the force that moves the universe off its course. But in an Author's Note that accompanies the play, Soyinka indicates his displeasure with this reading, which he calls "facile." For Soyinka, Simon's inability to understand is clearly present, but the focus of the play is on what happens to the universe when duty goes unfulfilled. Simon is simply an instrument or a "catalytic incident merely." Those who understand Yoruba belief can easily see the metaphysical confrontation in the play. For most Westerners, however, the recognizable conflict is between two religions, two races, two communities, and two cultures.

Duty and Responsibility

When Elesin heads toward death, he is repaying a debt. All his life he has enjoyed the company of the king, the finest clothes, "the choicest of the season's harvest." He has always known that he would follow the king in death, and as a man of honor he claims that he is eager for death and "will not delay." He knows his responsibility, and he accepts it. However, he is distracted at the end by the richness of the physical world. Rather than letting go of the world he draws it to him more closely, demanding finer clothing and one last sexual encounter.

His distraction proves his downfall. The ritual suicide is delayed while Elesin takes his new bride to bed, and the delay is enough time for Simon to have him arrested. The failure is Elesin's not Simon's, though Elesin tries to put the blame on the "alien race." Iyaloja rejects this interpretation. If

Elesin were strong enough in spirit, Simon could not keep him from his duty. Elesin is surrounded by others who fulfill their responsibilities: Iyaloja gives her son's bride-to-be to Elesin, Olunde travels all the way from England to bury his father and dies in his father's place, the bride closes her dead husband's eyes. Only Elesin fails, and the cost of his failure is high.

Style

Setting

Death and the King's Horseman takes place in the Nigerian town of Oyo in approximately 1943 or 1944. Nigeria became a colony of Great Britain in the nineteenth century, and into the 1940s British officers kept order and protected a small group of white Europeans who lived in the country. The white expatriates and the black Africans, members of the Yoruba people, inhabited parallel worlds, each group attempting to maintain its own traditional way of life.

The market is the center of the community, where people gather to socialize, to trade, to celebrate and to perform rituals, and it is here that Elesin comes as his last day draws to a close. The Western-style homes of the district officer and the resident are set apart from the village, but close enough that the sounds of the ceremonial drumming can be still be heard. The two communities, each holding a special event on the night of the play's action, do not mingle. No whites are present at the ceremony marking Elesin's passage, and the only blacks at the fancy-dress ball are servants.

Compare & Contrast

- **1940s:** Nigeria is a colony of Great

Britain, governed by a white British minority bureaucracy.

1963: Nigeria becomes an independent republic, with Nnamdi Azikiwe as first president.

1975: A military coup brings General Olusegun Obasanjo to power. He is Nigeria's third military dictator since 1966.

1999: The latest in a series of military rulers, General Abdulsalami Abubakar, assumes power and invites Soyinka back from a four-year exile. The general pledges to bring Nigeria out of its long period of oppression at the hands of corrupt military rulers.

- **1967:** Soyinka begins a prison term of more than two years for criticizing the Nigerian government. He will serve fifteen months in solitary confinement.

1974: Nobel-prize-winning author Aleksandr Solzhenitsyn is stripped of his Soviet citizenship and forced into exile. Writer Es'kia Mphahalele is living in exile from South Africa, after being arrested for protesting apartheid. Soyinka accepts a position as a visiting lecturer at Cambridge University in England.

2000: Solzhenitsyn, his citizenship restored, again lives in Russia. Mphahlele and Soyinka live in their home countries, where they are honored as intellectuals and political activists.

- **1970s:** African writing is not much taught in European or American schools, and is not widely read or understood outside Africa. When Soyinka is invited to be a visiting lecturer at Cambridge University, he is invited to talk about not literature, but about anthropology.

1986: Soyinka becomes the first African writer to be awarded the Nobel Prize for Literature. It is both an acknowledgment of his importance to world literature and an opportunity to attract even more readers around the world.

2000: High schools and colleges routinely offer courses in World Literature, and these courses increasingly include African and other so-called Third World literatures. Soyinka's plays, including *Death and the King's Horseman,* are frequently included in textbooks.

- **1953:** In the nation's first official

census, 43 percent of Nigerians report themselves as Muslims; 22 percent label themselves Christians; 34 percent are recorded as followers of ancestral religions.

1999: Fewer Nigerians now practice traditional religions. Approximately 50 percent are Muslims, 40 percent are Christian, and only 10 percent adhere to ancestral beliefs.

- **1945:** Few opportunities for higher education are available for blacks in Nigeria. Formal education consists mostly of missionary schools, and does not extend beyond the secondary level.

2000: Nigeria has an extensive system of public schools as well as many religious schools. There are several universities, and a few medical schools affiliated with teaching hospitals. Nigerians pursuing medical careers need not go abroad for their education.

Tragedy

In its structure, *Death and the King's Horseman* appears to be based on the tragedy. The tragedy is an ancient form of drama in which an important person passes through a series of events and choices, resulting in a great catastrophe. Tragedies have been written all around the world over thousands of years, to examine the dignity of humans and their greatest strengths and weaknesses. According to the ancient Greeks, tragedy filled the audience with fear and pity, and so helped a community deal psychologically with these emotions. The structure of a tragedy may be generally divided into several distinct parts: an introduction in which the characters, setting and situation are established; the complication or rising action, during which an opposing force is introduced; the climax or turning point; the falling action, or another focusing on the opposing forces; and the catastrophe, or the unhappy conclusion.

Death and the King's Horseman has in fact been built on this pattern. Act 1 introduces Elesin and his duty; Act 2 introduces an opposing force in the figure of Simon Pilkings, who plans to prevent Elesin's suicide; Act 3 ends with the climax of Elesin in transition, apparently only moments away from the central action, his death; Act 4 shifts the focus back to Simon Pilkings, and ends with the revelation that Elesin's suicide has been prevented; Act 5 contains Elesin's musings on the disorder brought about by his failure, and presents the deaths of Olunde and Elesin.

Foreshadowing

When a play or story includes early clues to

what will happen later, the writing is said to include foreshadowing. In *Death and the King's Horseman* there are several hints in Act 1 that Elesin will not carry through with his plan to commit suicide. As Elesin and the Praise-Singer enter the market, for example, Elesin comments on the attractiveness of the women there. The Praise-Singer agrees, but warns, "The hands of women also weaken the unwary." This warning creates in the audience's mind the possibility of failure, even danger. When Elesin promises that he will be faithful and join his forbears, the Praise-Singer replies, "In their time the world was never tilted from its groove, it shall not be in yours." Again, the possibility of failure is presented, as it will be several more times by the Praise-Singer and the women of the market as they assure each other that Elesin will not fail.

Elesin himself speaks eagerly about his determination to complete his duty. He dances and chants a long tale of the "Not-I bird," a bird who flew away when "Death came calling." Several critics have pointed out that Elesin seems here to be protesting too much. Why does he repeatedly assure the crowd that he will "not delay"? Why does he keep raising the specter of failure on what should be a glorious day of celebration? The foreshadowing helps prepare the audience for what will happen, prolonging and intensifying the experience of watching Elesin confront and then turn away from his duty.

Ritual

Death and the King's Horseman is set firmly in Yorubaland, and the metaphysical issues spring from Yoruba belief. However, as Nigeria and the rest of the world move "forward," the world becomes more homogenous and Western, and ancient beliefs and customs are lost. Soyinka writes in the Author's Note of the play's "threnodic essence," or the play's mourning the loss of tradition. With Elesin and Olunde both dead, the tradition of the king's horseman cannot continue, because it depends on the job of chief horseman being passed down from father to son. With Elesin's failure, an important ritual has been lost.

On stage, the play both celebrates and mourns ritual. Unlike the plays of William Shakespeare, which contain almost no stage directions, *Death and the King's Horseman* includes several lengthy passages in which the playwright describes what the actors are doing in addition to speaking their lines. Frequently, these stage directions describe elements of music, dance, and costume that are specific to Yoruba ritual. For example, Elesin parades into the market with an entourage of drummers and praise-singers, and the beginning of the play before a line is spoken—is a reenactment of part of the ritual of the horseman's last day. The stage directions also mandate that Elesin dance, accompanied by drumming, as he chants the story of the "Not-I bird"; that the *alari-cloth* the women drape him with be bright red and that they dance around him; that Simon and Jane dance the tango, and that they perform a sacrilegious imitation of the *egungun* ceremony; that Elesin dances his way into a trance;

and so on. These scenes are rich with sound and color, and most of them are not discussed by the characters. They form a separate layer of understanding, unavailable to those who merely read the printed script. In addition to the themes and ideas portrayed by the words the actors speak, the audience of a performance also witnesses a series of rituals enacted on stage as they used to be enacted in village markets.

A Nation in Turmoil

When Soyinka wrote *Death and the King's Horseman* in 1974 he was living in exile from Nigeria, lecturing at Churchill College of Cambridge University in England. The preceding years had been difficult for Nigeria, and for Soyinka personally. In 1967, the southeastern area of Nigeria declared itself the independent Republic of Biafra, and a civil war erupted. The causes of the conflict were complex: the secessionists were mostly from the Ibo tribe, and believed that the Nigerian government favored the Hausa tribe; many in the southeast were Christian, while those in the north were predominantly Muslim; oil was being produced in the region, and there was disagreement about how the revenues would be distributed.

Soyinka believed that the government policies toward Biafra were unjust, and he said as much in letters to the editors of national publications. Soyinka was arrested in 1967 and held without charges for two years and two months. For fifteen of those months, he was in solitary confinement. While he was in prison, the war continued, and the Biafrans were pushed to a smaller and smaller area of land. Shortly after Soyinka was released from prison in 1969, the war was over and Biafra had been completely wiped out. It was the first modern war between African blacks, and it left over one million people dead and many more homeless and starving. The Nigerian economy was in ruins; although profits from oil skyrocketed, most of the money was divided up between corrupt Nigerian military rulers and European oil companies, while the average Nigerian was unemployed and underfed.

After these experiences, Soyinka directed the University of Ibadan's Theatre Arts Department for a short time, and then lived mostly outside Nigeria for five years. He traveled throughout Europe and the United States, teaching, writing, and directing, and he spent two years as an editor in Ghana. According to many critics, his attention shifted after his imprisonment. Whereas previously he had written about the negative effects of the colonial powers on the colonized, he now addressed weakness and corruption wherever he found it. In particular, he was concerned with exploring the ways in which Africans treated each other unjustly, and the ways in which his own community had betrayed itself. *Death and the King's Horseman* is a play that reflects this later vision, as Soyinka himself insists in his Author's Note.

African Literature

African writers during the second half of the twentieth century faced a dilemma. Most of the traditional African forms of literature were based on oral traditional and ritual performance, and these ancient forms were becoming less and less familiar even to the local people. On the other hand, more widely popular genres like the novel and dramatic forms like the classical tragedy were based on European structures and philosophies, and did not always seem to fit African themes and beliefs. Language was also an issue: a play written in the local language would obviously capture the atmosphere and the spirit of a people better than the same story told in English, but the audience for such a play would be very limited.

Most of the African writers who are now considered major international figures traveled, taught, and produced important work in Europe and the United States, and they created works that combined European influences with African materials. With each new work they attempted to define what was "African" about African literature. Soyinka and others wrote eloquent essays in which they explored the place of Africa in world literature, and tried to determine how an African writer should make sense of various influences. Ngugi wa Thiong'o of Kenya, after several successful publications, decided to stop writing in English; since 1977 he has written his novels and plays in Gikuyu, but encouraged their publication in translation. Soyinka's works are written in English, but retain the original Yoruba for quoting certain proverbs, as in *Death and the King's Horseman*. However, in 1994 Akin Isola produced a translation of the play into Yoruba, as part of a new movement of Yoruba literature, a translation Soyinka endorsed.

Critical Overview

Death and the King's Horseman has been recognized from the beginning as an important work, but its critical reputation has been somewhat different in Nigeria than in Europe and the United States. Westerners have almost universally praised the play, and the Swedish Academy drew special attention to it in awarding Soyinka the 1986 Nobel Prize for Literature. Within Nigeria and within the community of Africans on the political left, however, some critics have quarreled with the play's political messages.

A central question answered differently by various critics and reviewers is the question of theme. What is the play about? Reviewers of performances of the play have tended to see the theme as the clash of cultures, focusing on the inability of the Pilkingses to understand Elesin and his responsibility. This is also how most audiences of performances have interpreted the play, as might be expected since most Western theater-goers do not bring much knowledge of Yoruba culture with them. In her study of the 1987 Lincoln Center production in New York, which Soyinka himself directed, Kacke Gotrick points out that even with Soyinka's Author's Note being reprinted in the *Playbill* and with Soyinka shaping every facet of the staging, some critics "nonetheless understood a cultural clash to be the central theme." Gotrick observes, as others have, that "Since Soyinka's drama relies on the Yoruba world-view, the interpreter's degree of knowledge of this world-view becomes decisive for his or her interpretation." The culture clash is also the theme analyzed by most Westerners who read the play, including high school and college students, as they also bring little knowledge of Yoruba to their reading experience.

Writers of scholarly articles and books, who have generally had the opportunity and the responsibility to learn more about Soyinka and about Yoruba cosmology, have been more likely to understand Soyinka's insistence that the clash of cultures is less important than the metaphysical examination of duty and ritual, and the representation of transition, a stage of the life cycle that connects the unborn, the living, and the dead. The theme of unfulfilled duty is explored in Derek Wright's *Wole Soyinka Revisited*. Wright examines the differences in plot between Soyinka's play and the historical events on which it is based, and points out Soyinka's own insistence that Simon Pilkings is only a catalyst. The emphasis is on the ritual that is not completed: "Elesin's failure to die, and so keep faith with his ancestors, spells the death of the ancestral past and the betrayal of the entire community of humans and spirits existing over the whole of time."

In his *Wole Soyinka: An Introduction to his Writing,* Obu Maduakor focuses on transition, the term Soyinka uses in the Author's Note. Maduakor describes Soyinka's cosmology, and concludes that "Elesin's bride represents the world of the living;

the seed implanted in her womb is a visitor from the world of the unborn. The dead Alafin, the 'King' of the play, has gone to the world of the dead, and Elesin himself is a creature of the twilight world of passage." Maduakor also traces Elesin's story, and demonstrates how it parallels the passage of Ogun, one of the Yoruba deities, through preparation, ritual death, and rebirth.

A major focus of criticism of *Death and the King's Horseman* has been providing assistance to readers who are not familiar with Yoruba culture. Much of the published criticism of the play offers little more than close reading, supported by helpful background information about the traditional role of the Praise-Singer, or the market, or the *egungun* ritual. An excellent example of this type of material is Bimpe Aboyade's *Wole Soyinka and Yoruba Oral Tradition* in *Death and the King's Horseman,* in which the writer explains the Yoruba oral traditions of the poets of the *egungun,* the hunters and the talking drum, and the aura of the ancestral masque. These cultural analyses are invaluable for Western readers or for African readers who are unfamiliar with Yoruba tradition.

Death and the King's Horseman has not been without detractors. Several critics have commented on the anachronistic situation presented by the play, observing that by the 1940s the failure of the king's horseman to commit ritual suicide would not have rocked the community. Some have found it difficult to accept that the European-educated Olunde would participate in the ritual. Other critics, particularly those in Nigeria, have written that Soyinka has romanticized the Yoruba, presenting them as more unified and tradition-bound than they are. African Marxist critics find that in emphasizing the cultural and religious differences between the British and the Yoruba, the play ignores essential class differences within Nigeria. Underlying much of the negative criticism is a sense that Soyinka's drama, influenced as it is by his study of drama around the world and also by study of Nigeria oral tradition, is simply not "African" enough. The universality that makes his plays so respected in Europe and North America is a sign, for some, that Soyinka has in many ways betrayed his own culture.

What Do I Read Next?

- *The Lion and the Jewel*(1963) is one of Soyinka' s earliest plays, and one of the first to be performed in Africa. More humorous than *Death and the King's Horseman,* it depicts a clash of cultures through the story of a confrontation between a schoolteacher and the village chief. As the two men try to win the hand of a beautiful woman, they argue the values of tradition and modernity.

- *Ake: The Years of Childhood*(1981) is Soyinka's second volume of memoir. Chosen by the *New York Times* as one of the twelve best books of 1982, it describes the first ten years of his life. Although Soyinka was something of a prodigy, beginning school at age three and becoming a teacher at ten, his gentle self-mocking humor makes the book delightful rather than self-serving.

- *The Handbook of Yoruba Religious Concepts*(1994) by Baba Ifa Karade presents clear and simple explanations of Yoruba beliefs and ceremonies. The presentation is not meant to win converts, but rather to strip away some of the mystery and make the traditions accessible to those who would wish to practice them or just to understand them. Karade also demonstrates similarities and differences between Yoruba and other spiritual beliefs.

- *The Palm-Wine Drinkard*(1953) by Amos Tutuola is a novel of a devoted West African drinker who undergoes a series of imaginative adventures. Tutuola built this humorous and dreamlike story out of traditional Yoruba folktales.

- *Things Fall Apart*(1958) is the first and most widely read novel by Nigerian writer Chinua Achebe, Through the story of Okonkwo, a member of the Ibo tribe, it depicts the changes in village life brought about when colonialism and Christianity intrud. Okonkwo is a complex character, not a simple victim of colonialism; his downfall comes both from forces within and from without.

- *Hamlet, Prince of Denmark,* a play written in approximately 1601 by William Shakespeare, is one of the most famous tragedies ever written. Prince Hamlet is the son of the king, who has just been murdered by Hamlet's uncle. The dead king urges Hamlet to revenge his death. Hamlet proves incapable of fulfilling his duty to the dead king, bringing chaos and death to himself and many of those close to him.

Sources

Gotrick, Kacke, "Soyinka and *Death and the King's Horseman,* or How Does Our Knowledge or Lack of Knowledge of Yoruba Culture Affect Our Interpretation?," in *Signs and Signals: Popular Culture in Africa,* edited by Raoul Granqvis, University of Umea, 1990, pp. 137, 139.

Maduakor, Obi, *Wole Soyinka: An Introduction to His Writing,* Garland, 1986, p. 273.

Mwagiru, Ciugu, "A Crusader's Return," in *World Press Review,* Vol. 46, no. 2, February 1999, p. 35.

Wright, Derek, *Wole Soyinka Revisited,* Twayne, 1993, p. 73.

Further Reading

Aboyade, Bimpe, *Wole Soyinka and Yoruba Oral Tradition,* in *Death and the King's Horseman,* Fountain Publications, 1994.

> A brief examination of the importance of oral tradition in Nigerian culture, and as a source for the play. Aboyade, himself a Yoruban, describes the *egungun* celebration, explains the role of the praise-singer, and considers the way in which Elesin and his people would understand honor.

Durosimi Jones, Eldred, *The Writing of Wole Soyinka,* 3d ed., Heinemann, 1988.

> The first edition of this volume, issued in 1973, was part of the Twayne World Authors Series, and for many years was considered the best book-length study of Soyinka. The third edition is still strong on the early years and early works, and on Soyinka's incorporation of Christian and Yoruba elements, but the discussions of later plays, including *Death and the King's Horseman,* are brief.

Gibbs, James, ed., *Critical Perspectives on Wole*

Soyinka, Three Continents Press, 1980.

> A collection of critical essays on Soyinka's plays, poetry, memoir and criticism from a variety of perspectives. The book is now somewhat dated, and many of these essays may be difficult for the general reader, but the essays are consistently insightful and the collection is thorough.

Gotrick, Kacke, "Soyinka and *Death and the King's Horseman,* or How Does Our Knowledge or Lack of Knowledge of Yoruba Culture Affect Our Interpretation?," in *Signs and Signals: Popular Culture in Africa,* edited by Raoul Granqvist, University of Umea, 1990, pp. 137-148.

> Gotrick delineates the two major interpretations of the play as Elesin's failure or as a clash of cultures and concludes that readers and viewers are likely to choose an interpretation based on their level of "Yoruba competence." The analysis is based on the 1987 New York production, and the article includes three photographs from that production.

Levy, Patricia, *Nigeria,* Marshall Cavendish, 1996. Part of the Cultures of the World series, this volume is intended for middle school and high school students. Accessible but substantial, it gives an objective overview of Nigeria's history and geography, and explores the religions, languages, arts and festivals of the major ethnic groups. The many colored pictures illustrate dramatically the ways in which Nigeria is like and unlike North America.

Maduakor, Obi, *Wole Soyinka: An Introduction to His Writing,* Garland, 1986.

> This volume is intended to make Soyinka more accessible to Western students by explaining the playwright's world view, his use of mythology, and his use of language. Maduakor analyzes *Death and the King's Horseman* as a play about transition from one spiritual world to another, paralleling the passage of the hero-god Ogun.

Wright, Derek, *Wole Soyinka Revisited,* Twayne, 1993.

> An excellent introduction to Soyinka's life and work, with an emphasis on Yoruban traditions and themes as they inform Soyinka's writing. Wright's discussion of *Death and the King's Horseman* focuses on the changes Soyinka made to the actual historical events, demonstrating how these changes reinforce the themes of interrupted ritual and substitution.

CPSIA information can be obtained
at www.ICGtesting.com
Printed in the USA
BVHW031301210822
645119BV00013B/1076

9 781375 378666